THE THIRTY-NINE STEPS

As Richard Hannay walks home to his flat in London, he is feeling bored. Nothing exciting ever seems to happen in England, he thinks. Perhaps he'll go back to Africa. But that night he has a visitor, a man called Scudder, who has a strange story to tell.

A week later Hannay is lying, hungry and exhausted, in the heather on a Scottish moor. Above him a small plane circles in the blue sky, flying low. Hannay lies still, hoping desperately that the plane will not see him, and thinks about Scudder's little black notebook in his pocket. Who are the people chasing him – the mysterious 'Black Stone' that Scudder writes about? What is so important about 'the thirty-nine steps'? And what is going to happen in London on the 15th of June?

But Scudder has been murdered, and Hannay must find his own answers, while his enemies chase him night and day through the hills of Scotland. If they catch him, they will kill him . . .

OXFORD BOOKWORMS LIBRARY
Thriller & Adventure

The Thirty-Nine Steps

Stage 4 (1400 headwords)

Series Editor: Jennifer Bassett
Founder Editor: Tricia Hedge
Activities Editors: Jennifer Bassett and Alison Baxter

JOHN BUCHAN

The Thirty-Nine Steps

Retold by
Nick Bullard

OXFORD UNIVERSITY PRESS

OXFORD
UNIVERSITY PRESS

Great Clarendon Street, Oxford OX2 6DP

Oxford University Press is a department of the University of Oxford.
It furthers the University's objective of excellence in research, scholarship,
and education by publishing worldwide in

Oxford New York

Auckland Cape Town Dar es Salaam Hong Kong Karachi
Kuala Lumpur Madrid Melbourne Mexico City Nairobi
New Delhi Shanghai Taipei Toronto

With offices in

Argentina Austria Brazil Chile Czech Republic France Greece
Guatemala Hungary Italy Japan Poland Portugal Singapore
South Korea Switzerland Thailand Turkey Ukraine Vietnam

OXFORD and OXFORD ENGLISH are registered trade marks of
Oxford University Press in the UK and in certain other countries

ISBN 978 0 19 479188 5

A complete recording of this Bookworms edition of
. The Thirty-Nine Steps is available on audio CD ISBN 978 0 19 479156 4

Typeset by Wyvern Typesetting Ltd, Bristol

Printed in Hong Kong

ACKNOWLEDGEMENTS
Illustrated by: Ron Tiner

Word count (main text): 17,170 words

For more information on the Oxford Bookworms Library,
visit www.oup.com/elt/bookworms

CONTENTS

THE MAN WHO DIED

I returned to my flat at about three o'clock on that May afternoon very unhappy with life. I had been back in Britain for three months and I was already bored. The weather was bad, the people were dull, and the amusements of London seemed as exciting as a glass of cold water. 'Richard Hannay,' I told myself, 'you have made a mistake, and you had better do something about it.'

It made me angry when I thought of the years I had spent in Africa. I had spent those years working very hard and making money. Not a lot of money, but enough for me. I had left Scotland when I was six years old, and I had never been home since. For years I had dreamt of coming home to Britain and spending the rest of my life there, but I was disappointed with the place after the first week. And so here I was, thirty-seven years old, healthy, with enough money to have a good time, and bored to death.

That evening I went out to dinner and sat reading the newspapers afterwards. They were full of the troubles in south-east Europe, and there was a long report about Karolides, the Greek Prime Minister. He seemed to be an honest man, but some people in Europe hated him. However, many people in Britain liked him, and one newspaper said that he was the only man who could prevent a war starting. I remember wondering if I could get a job in south-east Europe; it might be a lot less boring than life in London.

As I walked home that night, I decided to give Britain one

more day. If nothing interesting happened, I would take the next boat back to Africa.

My flat was in a big new building in Langham Place. There was a doorman at the entrance to the building, but each flat was separate, with its own front door. I was just putting the key into my door when a man appeared next to me. He was thin, with a short brown beard and small, very bright eyes. I recognized him as the man who lived in a flat on the top floor of the building. We had spoken once or twice on the stairs.

'Can I speak to you?' he asked. 'May I come in for a minute?' His voice was shaking a little.

I opened the door and we went in.

'Is the door locked?' he asked, and quickly locked it himself.

'I'm very sorry,' he said to me. 'It's very rude of me. But I'm in a dangerous corner and you looked like the kind of man who would understand. If I explain, will you help me?'

'I'll listen to you,' I said. 'That's all I promise.' I was getting worried by this strange man's behaviour.

There was a table with drinks on it next to him, and he took a large whisky for himself. He drank it quickly, and then put the glass down so violently that it broke.

'I'm sorry,' he said. 'I'm a little nervous tonight. You see, at this moment I'm dead.'

I sat down in an armchair and lit my pipe.

'How does it feel?' I asked. I was now almost sure that the man was mad.

He smiled. 'I'm not mad – yet. Listen, I've been watching you, and I guess that you're not easily frightened. I'm going to tell you my story. I need help very badly, and I want to know if you're the right man to ask.'

'Tell me your story,' I said, 'and I'll tell you if I can help you.'

It was an extraordinary story. I didn't understand all of it, and I had to ask a lot of questions, but here it is:

His name was Franklin P. Scudder and he was an American, but he had been in south-east Europe for several years. By accident, he had discovered a group of people who were working secretly to push Europe towards a war. These people were clever, and dangerous. Some of them wanted to change the world through war; others simply wanted to make a lot of money, and there is always money to be made from a war. Their plan was to get Russia and Germany at war with each other.

'I want to stop them,' Scudder told me, 'and if I can stay alive for another month, I think I can.'

'I thought you were already dead,' I said.

'I'll tell you about that in a minute,' he answered. 'But first, do you know who Constantine Karolides is?'

'The Greek Prime Minister. I've just been reading about him in today's newspapers.'

'Right. He's the only man who can stop the war. He's intelligent, he's honest, and he knows what's going on – and so his enemies plan to kill him. I have discovered how. That was very dangerous for me, so I had to disappear. They can't kill Karolides in Greece because he has too many guards. But on the 15th of June he's coming to London for a big meeting, and his enemies plan to kill him here.'

'You can warn him,' I said. 'He'll stay at home.'

'That's what his enemies want. If he doesn't come, they'll win, because he's the only man who understands the whole problem and who can stop the war happening.'

'Why don't you go to the British police?' I said.

'No good. They could bring in five hundred policemen, but they wouldn't stop the murder. The murderer will be caught, and he'll talk and put the blame on the governments in Vienna and Berlin. It will all be lies, of course, but everybody will be ready to believe it. But none of this will happen if Franklin P. Scudder is here in London on the 15th of June.'

I was beginning to like this strange little man. I gave him another whisky and asked him why he thought that he was now in danger himself.

He took a large mouthful of whisky. 'I came to London by a strange route – through Paris, Hamburg, Norway, and Scotland. I changed my name in every country, and when I got to London, I thought I was safe. But yesterday I realized that they're still following me. There's a man watching this building and last night somebody put a card under my door. On it was the name of the man I fear most in the world.

'So I decided I had to die. Then they would stop looking for me. I got a dead body – it's easy to get one in London, if you know how – and I had the body brought to my flat in a large suitcase. The body was the right age, but the face was different from mine. I dressed it in my clothes and shot it in the face with my own gun. My servant will find me when he arrives in the morning and he'll call the police. I've left a lot

I was beginning to like this strange little man.

of empty whisky bottles in my room. The police will think I drank too much and then killed myself.' He paused. 'I watched from the window until I saw you come home, and then came down the stairs to meet you.'

It was the strangest of stories. However, in my experience, the most extraordinary stories are often the true ones. And if the man just wanted to get into my flat and murder me, why didn't he tell a simpler story?

'Right,' I said. 'I'll trust you for tonight. I'll lock you in this room and keep the key. Just one word, Mr Scudder. I believe you're honest, but if you're not, I should warn you that I know how to use a gun.'

'Certainly,' he answered, jumping up. 'I'm afraid I don't know your name, sir, but I would like to thank you. And could I use your bathroom?'

When I next saw him, half an hour later, I didn't recognize him at first. Only the bright eyes were the same. His beard was gone, and his hair was completely different. He walked like a soldier, and he was wearing glasses. And he no longer spoke like an American.

'Mr Scudder—' I cried.

'Not Mr Scudder,' he answered. 'Captain Theophilus Digby of the British Army. Please remember that.'

I made him a bed in my study, and then went to bed myself, happier than I had been for the past month. Interesting things did happen sometimes, even in London.

* * *

The next morning when my servant Paddock arrived, I introduced him to Captain Digby. I explained that the Captain was an important man in the army, but he had been working too hard and needed rest and quiet. Then I went out, leaving them both in the flat. When I returned at about lunchtime, the doorman told me that the gentleman in flat 15 had killed himself. I went up to the top floor, had a few words with the police, and was able to report to Scudder that his plan had been successful. The police believed that the dead man was Scudder, and that he had killed himself. Scudder was very pleased.

For the first two days in my flat, he was very calm, and spent all his time reading and smoking, and writing in a little black notebook. But after that he became more restless and nervous. It was not his own danger that he worried about, but the success of his plan to prevent the murder of Karolides. One night he was very serious.

'Listen, Hannay,' he said. 'I think I must tell you some more about this business. I would hate to get killed without leaving someone else to carry on with my plan.'

I didn't listen very carefully. I was interested in Scudder's adventures, but I wasn't very interested in politics. I remember that he said Karolides was only in danger in London. He also mentioned a woman called Julia Czechenyi. He talked about a Black Stone and a man who lisped when he spoke. And he described another man, perhaps the most dangerous of them all – an old man with a young voice who could hood his eyes like a hawk.

The next evening I had to go out. I was meeting a man I had known in Africa for dinner. When I returned to the flat, I was surprised to see that the light in the study was out. I wondered if Scudder had gone to bed early. I turned on the light, but there was nobody there. Then I saw something in the corner that made my blood turn cold.

Scudder was lying on his back. There was a long knife through his heart, pinning him to the floor.

There was a long knife through Scudder's heart.

2

THE MILKMAN STARTS HIS TRAVELS

I sat down in an armchair and felt very sick. After about five minutes I started shaking. The poor white face with its staring eyes was too much for me, so I got a table-cloth and covered it. Then I took the whisky bottle and drank several mouthfuls. I had seen men die violently before. I had killed a few myself in the Matabele war; but this was different. After a few more minutes I managed to calm myself down a little. I looked at my watch and saw that it was half-past ten. I searched the flat carefully, but there was nobody there. Then I locked the doors and windows.

By this time I was beginning to think more clearly. It looked bad for me – that was clear. It was now certain that Scudder's story was true – the proof was lying under the table-cloth. His enemies had found him and made sure of his silence. But he had been in my flat for four days, and they must think he had told his story to me. So I would be the next to die. It might be that night, or the next day, or the day after, but it was sure to happen.

Then I thought of another problem. I could call the police now, or go to bed and wait for Paddock to discover the body and call them in the morning. But what would the police think? What story would I tell them about Scudder? I had lied to Paddock about him, and my story would be hard to believe. They would arrest me for murder, and I had no real friends in England to help me. Perhaps that was part of the plan. An English prison would be a safe place for me until the 15th of June.

Even if the police did believe my story, I would still be helping Scudder's enemies. Karolides would stay at home, which was what they wanted. Scudder's death had made me certain that his story was true; now I felt responsible for continuing his work. I hate to see a good man beaten, and if I carried on in Scudder's place, the murderers might not win.

I decided I must disappear, and remain hidden until just

before the 15th of June. Then I must contact some government people and tell them Scudder's story. I wished he had told me more, and that I had listened more carefully to what he had told me. There was a risk that the government would not believe me, but it was my best chance. Perhaps more evidence would appear which would help me to make my story believable.

It was now the 24th of May, so I had twenty days of hiding. Two groups of people would be looking for me – Scudder's enemies, who would want to kill me, and the police, who would want me for Scudder's murder. There was going to be a chase, and, surprisingly, I was almost happy about this. I did not want to sit in one place and wait. If I could move, the situation did not seem so bad.

I wondered if Scudder had any papers which would give me more information about his business. I lifted off the table-cloth and searched him. There were only a few coins in his trouser pockets. There was no sign of the little black notebook. I supposed his murderer had taken that.

When I turned from the body, I noticed that all the cupboards were open. Scudder had been a very careful man, and always kept the place tidy. Someone had been searching for something, and perhaps for the notebook. I went round the flat and found that everything had been searched – the insides of books, cupboards, boxes, even the pockets of my clothes. There was no sign of the notebook, so Scudder's enemies had probably found it in the end.

Then I got out a map of Britain. My plan was to find some wild country. I was used to Africa, and I would feel trapped in the city. I thought Scotland would probably be best, because my family came from Scotland and I could pretend to be a Scotsman easily. The other possibility was to be a German tourist; my father had worked with Germans and I had spoken German often as a boy. But it would probably be better to be a Scotsman in Scotland. I decided to go to Galloway, which, from the map, seemed to be the nearest wild part of Scotland.

In the railway timetable I found a train from London at seven-ten in the morning, which would get me to Galloway in the late afternoon. The problem was getting to the station, as I was certain that Scudder's enemies were watching the building. I thought about this problem, had a good idea, went to bed, and slept for two hours.

I got up at four o'clock. The first light of a summer morning was in the sky and the birds were starting to sing. I put on some old clothes which I used for country walking and some strong walking boots. I pushed another shirt and a toothbrush into my pockets. I had taken a lot of money out of the bank in case Scudder needed it, so I took that as well. Then I cut my long moustache as short as possible.

Paddock arrived every morning at seven-thirty. But at about twenty to seven I knew the milkman would come; the noise of the milk bottles usually woke me up. He was a young man with a very short moustache, and he wore a white coat. He was my only chance.

I had a breakfast of biscuits and whisky and by the time I had finished it was about six o'clock. I got my pipe and started to fill it from my tobacco jar. As I put my fingers into the tobacco, I touched something hard, and pulled out Scudder's little black book.

This seemed a good sign. I lifted the cloth and looked at Scudder's peaceful face. 'Goodbye, my friend,' I said; 'I'm going to do my best for you. Wish me good luck.'

Six-thirty passed, then six-forty, but still the milkman did not come. Why, oh why, was this the morning he had to be late?

At fourteen minutes to seven I heard him. I opened the door quickly, and he jumped a bit when he saw me.

'Come in a moment,' I said, and we went back into the hall. 'I can see you're a man who likes a bit of fun. Can you help me? Lend me your hat and coat for a minute and you can have this.'

He looked at the money in my hand and smiled. 'What do you want my clothes for?' he asked.

'It's a game,' I said. 'I haven't time to explain now, but to win I've got to be a milkman for ten minutes. You'll be a bit late, but you'll get the money for your time.'

'All right!' he said. 'I like a game myself. Here you are.'

I put on his blue hat and white coat, picked up the empty milk bottles, shut my door and went downstairs, whistling.

At first I thought the street was empty. Then I saw a man walking slowly towards me. As he passed, he looked up at a window in the house opposite, and I saw a face look back at him.

I crossed the street, still whistling, and then turned down a little side street. As I dropped the hat, coat and milk bottles behind a wall, I heard a church clock; it was seven o'clock.

I ran to the station as fast as I could. It was just ten past seven when I reached the platform. I had no time to buy a

I put on the milkman's hat and coat.

ticket; the train was already moving. I jumped into the last carriage.

3

THE HOTEL-OWNER

It was fine May weather as I travelled north that day, and as I watched the fields and the trees and the flowers, I wondered why, when I had been a free man, I had stayed in London. I bought some sandwiches at lunch time. I also bought the morning newspaper and read a little about south-east Europe.

When I had finished, I got out Scudder's black book and studied it. It was almost full of writing, mostly numbers, although sometimes there was a name. For example, I found the words 'Hofgaard', 'Luneville', and 'Avocado' quite often. The word I saw the most was 'Pavia'.

I was certain that Scudder was using a code. I have always been interested in codes; I enjoy games and numbers and things like that. It seemed to be a number code, where groups of numbers replace letters. I worked on the words, because you can use a word as a key in a number code.

I tried for hours, but none of the words helped. Then I fell asleep, and woke up at Dumfries just in time to take the local train into Galloway. There was a man on the platform who worried me a little; he was watching the crowd more closely than I liked. But he didn't look at me, and when I saw myself in a mirror, I understood why; with my brown face and my old clothes I looked just like all the other hill farmers who were getting into the local train.

I travelled with a group of these farmers. The train travelled slowly through narrow valleys and then up onto an open moor. There were lakes, and in the distance I could see high mountains.

At five o'clock the carriage was empty and I was alone. I got out at the next station, a tiny place in the middle of the moor. An old man was digging in the station garden. He stopped, walked to the train, collected a packet, and went back to his potatoes. A ten-year-old child took my ticket, and I came out of the station onto a white road across the moor.

It was a beautiful, clear spring evening. I felt like a boy on a walking holiday, instead of a man of thirty-seven very much wanted by the police. I walked along that road whistling, feeling happier every minute.

After some time I left the road and followed a path along a little stream. I was getting tired when I came to a small house. The woman who lived there was friendly, and said I could sleep there. She also gave me an excellent meal.

Her husband came home from the hills later in the evening. We talked about cows and sheep and markets, and I tried to remember some of the information I heard, because it might be useful. By ten o'clock I was asleep, and I slept until five o'clock in the morning.

The couple refused any money, and by six o'clock I had eaten breakfast and was moving again. I wanted to get back to the railway at a different station. Then I would go back to the east, towards Dumfries. I hoped that if the police were following me, they would think that I had gone on to the coast in the west, where I could escape by ship.

I walked in the same beautiful spring weather as before, and still couldn't make myself feel nervous or worried. After a time I came to the railway line, and soon a little station, which was perfect for my plan. There was just a single line and moors all around. I waited until I saw a train in the distance, and then bought a ticket to Dumfries.

The only person in the carriage was an old farmer with his sheepdog. He was asleep, and next to him was a newspaper. I picked it up to see if there was any news about me. There was only a short piece about the Langham Place Murder. My servant Paddock had called the police, and the milkman had been arrested. The poor man had spent most of the day with the police, but they had let him go in the evening. The police believed that the real murderer had escaped from London on a train to the north.

When I had finished reading, I looked out of the window and noticed that we were stopping at the station where I had got out yesterday. Three men were talking to the man who I had seen digging potatoes. I sat well back from the window and watched carefully. One of the men was taking notes, and I supposed they were from the local police. Then, I saw the child who had taken my ticket talking, and the men looked out across the moor along the road I had taken.

As we left the station, the farmer woke up, looked at me, and asked where he was. He had clearly drunk too much.

'I'm like this because I never drink,' he said, sadly. 'I haven't touched whisky since last year. Not even at

Christmas. And now I've got this terrible headache.'

'What did it?' I asked.

'A drink they call brandy. I didn't touch the whisky because I don't drink, but I kept drinking this brandy. I'll be ill for a fortnight.' His voice got slower and slower and soon he fell asleep again.

I had planned to leave the train at a station, but it now stopped by a river and I decided this would be better. I looked out of the carriage window and saw nobody, so I opened the door and dropped quickly down into the long grass. My plan was going perfectly until the dog decided that I was stealing something and began to bark loudly. This woke up the farmer who started to shout. He thought I was trying to kill myself. I crawled through the long grass for about a hundred metres and then looked back. The train driver and several passengers were all staring in my direction.

Luckily, the dog was now so excited that he pulled the farmer out of the carriage. The farmer began to slide down towards the river. The other passengers ran to help him, the dog bit somebody, and there was a lot of excited shouting. Soon they had forgotten me, and the next time I looked back, the train was moving again.

I was now in the middle of the empty moor, and for the first time I felt really frightened, not of the police but of the people who knew that I knew Scudder's secret. If they caught me, I would be a dead man.

I reached the top of a low hill and looked around. To the south, a long way away, I saw something which made me tremble . . .

My plan was going perfectly until the dog began to bark.

Low in the sky a small plane was flying slowly across the moor. I was certain that it was looking for me, and I was also certain that it was not the police. I hid low in the heather and watched it for an hour or two as it flew in circles. Finally it disappeared to the south.

I did not like this spying from the air, and I began to think that an open moor was perhaps not the best place to hide. I could see distant forests in the east, and decided that would be better country.

It was about six o'clock in the evening when I left the moor and entered the trees. I came to a bridge by a house, and there, on the bridge, was a young man. He was sitting smoking a pipe, dreamily watching the water, and holding a book. He jumped up as he heard my feet on the road and I saw a friendly young face.

'Good evening to you,' he said in a serious voice. 'It's a fine night to be on the road.'

The smell of cooking came from the house.

'Is that house a hotel?' I asked.

'It certainly is. I'm the owner, and I hope you'll stay the night, because I've been alone for a week.'

I sat down next to him and got out my pipe. I began to think this young man might help me.

'You're young to own a hotel,' I said.

'My father died a year ago and now it's mine. It's not an exciting job for a young man like me. I didn't choose to do it. I want to write books.'

'You've got the right job,' I said. 'With all the travellers you meet you could be the best storyteller in the world.'

'Not today,' he said. 'Two hundred years ago, there were

exciting people on the road, but today there are only cars full of fat old women, and fishermen. You can't make stories out of them. I want to sail up an African river, or live in an Indian village – and write about things like that.'

The hotel looked peaceful in the evening sun.

'I've travelled a bit,' I said, 'and I'd be happy to live in a peaceful place like this. And perhaps you're sitting next to adventure now. I'll tell you a true story, and you can make a book of it if you like.'

I told him I was in the gold business in Africa, and I had discovered a group of international thieves. They had chased me to England and had killed my best friend. I described a chase across the desert, and an attack on the ship from Africa. And I described the Langham Place murder in detail. 'You want adventure,' I said, 'well, here it is. The thieves are chasing me now, and the police are chasing them.'

'It's wonderful!' he whispered.

'You believe me,' I said gratefully.

'Of course I do,' he said. 'I can believe anything strange. It's things that happen every day that are difficult to believe.'

He was very young, but he was the man I needed.

'I think my enemies have lost me for the moment. But I must hide and rest for a day or two. Will you help me?'

He jumped up and led me to the house. 'You'll be safe here. I can keep a secret. And you'll tell me some more about your adventures, won't you?'

As I entered the hotel, I heard the sound of an engine. In the sky to the west was my enemy the plane.

He gave me a room at the back of the house. I asked him to watch out for cars and planes and sat down to work on Scudder's little book. As I have said, it was a number code. I had to find the word that was the key to it, and when I thought of the million words it might be, I felt hopeless. But the next afternoon I remembered that Scudder had said a woman called Julia Czechenyi was the key to the Karolides business, so I tried her name as the code key.

It was the answer. In half an hour I was reading, with a white face.

Suddenly, I heard the sound of a car stopping outside the hotel.

Ten minutes later, my young friend came up to my room, his eyes bright with excitement.

'There are two men looking for you,' he whispered. 'They're downstairs now having a drink. They described you very well. I told them you had stayed here last night and had left this morning.'

I asked him to describe them. One was a thin man with dark eyes, the other was always smiling and lisped. They were both English; my young friend was certain of this.

I took a piece of paper and wrote these words in German. I made it look like one page of a private letter:

... *Black Stone. Scudder had discovered this, but he could do nothing for a fortnight. I don't think it's any good now because Karolides is uncertain about his plans. But if Mr T. advises, I will do the best I ...*

'Give this to them and say you found it in my bedroom. Ask them to return it to me if they find me.'

Three minutes later the car began to move. From behind

'*That paper woke them up. The thin man went white,
and the fat one whistled.*'

the curtain I saw two men in it, one thin, one fatter.

The young man came back. He was very excited. 'That paper woke them up,' he said, happily. 'The thin man went white, and the fat one whistled. Then they left as quickly as they could.'

'Now I'll tell you what I want you to do,' I said. 'Go to the police station and describe the two men to them. Say you think they may have something to do with the London murder. I'm sure those two men will be back here tomorrow morning for more information about me. Tell the police to be here early.'

At about eight o'clock the next morning I watched three policemen arrive. They hid their car and came into the hotel. Twenty minutes later another car came towards the hotel, but stopped in some trees about two hundred metres away. The two men inside walked up to the hotel.

I had planned to hide in my bedroom and see what happened. But now I had a better idea. I wrote a note to thank the young man for his help, opened my window and dropped out. Watching the hotel carefully, I walked back towards the car in the trees, jumped in, and drove away.

4

THE POLITICAL CANDIDATE

I drove that car across the moor as fast as I could, looking nervously over my shoulder. I was also thinking desperately about Scudder's notes.

Scudder had told me nothing but lies. All his stories about south-east Europe and people wanting to start wars were rubbish. But although he had told me lies, there was truth underneath.

The 15th of June was going to be an important day, but because of something more important than the murder of a Prime Minister. The story in his book was not complete, and there were some things I didn't understand – for example, the words 'thirty-nine steps', which appeared five or six times. The last time the words were used, Scudder had written 'Thirty-nine steps, I counted them – high tide at 10.17 p.m.'

The first thing I learned was that war was certain. Everything was planned. Karolides was going to be murdered and nothing could prevent it.

The second thing I learned was that Britain was not prepared for war. Karolides would be murdered and war would seem certain. Germany would pretend to be against war, but while we and they discussed peace, their submarines would silently fill the seas around us.

There was something else. Although the newspapers didn't know it, the British and French governments were close allies, and had agreed to prepare for war together. The most important officers in the armies and navies met regularly, and in June one of the top people was coming from Paris for a meeting. He would be told the exact details of the British Navy's preparations for war.

But on the 15th of June other people were going to be in London. Scudder didn't give names, but called them just the 'Black Stone'. They had a plan to get hold of this information, which was meant only for the French Government. And the information would be used by our enemies just a week or two later, with a most terrible effect.

My first idea was to write a letter to the British Prime Minister. But nobody would believe my story. I had to find proof that Scudder's story was true; and this would not be easy with the police and the Black Stone following me.

I drove to the east through a country at peace; but I knew that in a month's time, unless I was very lucky, men would be lying dead in this quiet countryside. I came into a village and I saw a policeman standing outside the Post Office and reading something carefully. He looked up at the car, stepped into the road, and held up a hand to stop me.

I almost did stop. But then I realized that the policeman had been reading about me. I supposed the police at the hotel had worked quickly and contacted all the local villages. I drove faster, the policeman jumped out of my way, and I was soon out of the village.

I left the main road as soon as possible and tried a smaller one. It was not easy without a map, and I realized that I had been stupid to steal the car. It would help the police and the Black Stone to find me in any corner of Scotland. If I left it, and went off on foot, they would find me in an hour or two.

I took a road that went along a narrow valley, and then up onto the moor again. I was very hungry; I had eaten nothing since morning. And now, as I drove, I heard a noise in the sky, and there was the plane.

On the moor it would see me in a minute. I drove as fast as I could down into another valley and towards a wood. Suddenly, a car appeared in front of me from a side road.

The car began to fall. I jumped out and was caught by a tree.

There was no time to stop. I did the only thing possible and drove off the road into a hedge, hoping to hit something soft beyond. But I was out of luck. The car went through the hedge like a knife through butter, and immediately began to fall. I jumped out and was caught by the branch of a tree, while the car disappeared into a river fifteen metres below.

* * *

A hand helped me out of the tree, and a frightened voice asked me if I was badly hurt. The speaker was a young man who was very alarmed and very sorry. I was more pleased than angry; it was a good way for the car to disappear.

'It's my fault,' I told him. 'That's the end of my holiday, but that's better than the end of my life!'

He looked at his watch. 'I'm in a hurry, but my house is very near. Let me give you some food and a bed. But what about your luggage? Is it in the river?'

'It's in my pocket,' I said. 'I'm from Australia, so I never carry much luggage.'

'From Australia,' he cried. 'You're just the man I need.'

We got into his car and in three minutes we were at his very comfortable house. He found some food for me. 'You've only got five minutes, I'm afraid, but you can eat properly afterwards. We've got to be at the meeting at eight o'clock. You see, I'm a candidate for the election and I've got a problem tonight. I had arranged for Crumpleton, who was the Australian Prime Minister, to speak at the meeting tonight, but he's ill. I've got to speak for forty minutes, and I don't know what to say. Listen, Mr – you haven't told me your name – Twisdon, you say? Well, Mr

Twisdon, can you talk about Australia for a few minutes?'

It seemed strange to ask a man you had met in a car crash to speak at an election meeting, but I needed his help.

'All right,' I said. 'I'm not a good speaker, but I'll speak for a bit.'

He was delighted. We got in his car, and on the way to the meeting he told me about his life. His name was Sir Harry Andrews and his uncle was in the government and had suggested politics as a job. He knew nothing about politics, but he was a friendly young man and I was glad to help him. When we arrived at the meeting, there were about five hundred people waiting. I was introduced as a 'trusted Australian leader' and then Sir Harry started to speak. It was mostly about preparing for war. He said the Germans didn't want a war and that if we stopped building new warships, the Germans would do the same. I thought about Scudder's black book in my pocket.

But behind all the rubbish I could see that Sir Harry was a nice man. And he spoke very badly. I knew I wasn't a good speaker, but I would be better than him.

I simply told them everything I knew about Australia. I said that Britain and Australia must work together and be friends. I think I was rather a success.

When we were back in his car again, Sir Harry was delighted. 'You spoke wonderfully, Twisdon,' he said. 'Now you must stay for a few days. There's excellent fishing here.'

We had a good supper – which I needed – and sat in front of a fire in his sitting-room. I thought the time had come for me to tell the truth and see if this man could help me.

'Listen, Sir Harry, I've got something very important to say to you. You're an honest man, and I'm going to be honest too. Everything you said tonight was dangerous rubbish.'

'Was it? I wasn't sure myself. Do you think Germany is going to start a war with us?'

'In six weeks' time you won't need to ask me that. Listen, and I'll tell you a story.'

I sat in front of the fire, in that peaceful room, and told him everything. He heard about Scudder, his notebook, the milkman, and my travels in Scotland. It was the first time I had told the truth, all of it, to anyone, and I felt better.

'So you see,' I said finally, 'I'm the man the police want for the Langham Place murder. You should call them at once.'

He looked at me carefully. 'I know you're not a murderer, Hannay, and I believe you're speaking the truth. I'll help you. What do you want me to do?'

'First, write to your uncle. I must contact the government before the 15th of June.'

He pulled his moustache. 'That won't help you. My uncle isn't interested in foreign politics, and I don't think he'd believe you. No. I'll write to a friend of his, Sir Walter Bullivant, who works in the Foreign Office. He's an intelligent man and I think he'd help. What shall I say?'

So he wrote a letter to Sir Walter, saying that if a man named Twisdon came to him, he should help him. Twisdon would say the words 'Black Stone' and would whistle the song 'Annie Laurie', to prove who he was.

He told me where Sir Walter lived, and asked me what

more he could do.

'Can you lend me some old clothes and give me a map? And if the police come, show them the car in the river.'

I then slept for three or four hours, until Sir Harry woke me at two o'clock. He gave me an old bicycle for the first part of the journey.

5

THE ADVENTURE OF THE ROADMAN

I sat down at the top of a hill and rested. Behind me was a road climbing out of a river valley. In front were two kilometres of flat open country. To the left and the right were green hills. A kilometre down the road behind me I could see the smoke from a small house, but otherwise there was no sign of human life. There were only the sounds of birds singing and water flowing.

It was now about seven o'clock in the morning, and as I waited, I heard the sound of an engine in the air. I realized that I was in a bad position, because I had nowhere to hide.

I sat, hopelessly, as the aeroplane came nearer. It was high at first, but then it came down very low. I could see one of the two men looking at me very carefully. Then, suddenly, it went up and disappeared.

I had to think quickly. My enemies had found me, so now, I supposed, they would put a circle of men around the hills. They had probably seen my bicycle, so they would expect me to try and escape by road. I found a small lake about a hundred metres from the road and threw the bicycle in. Then I climbed to a higher bit of ground and looked around.

There was nowhere to hide. The moor was open, but to me it was like a prison. I started to walk to the north, and as I walked, I saw a car about fifteen kilometres away on the road. And, in the valley below me, I could see a line of men walking slowly upwards. The north was no good. I turned, and began to run southwards. I ran hard, watching the skyline in front of me, and soon I thought I could see distant figures on the hill. I turned again and ran down to the road.

If you have enemies all around you, the best plan is to hide while they search and do not find you. But there was

The moor was open, but to me it was like a prison.

nothing to hide in, nothing but the moor, the heather, and the white road.

* * *

Then, in a bend in the road, I found the roadman. He had just started work mending the road, when he saw me.

'I'm sorry I ever stopped farming!' he said. 'I was my own boss then. Now I have to do what the government orders, and I'm a prisoner here with aching eyes and a bad back. And my head's going to explode!'

He was about the same age as me, and wore big black glasses. He started to work again, and then stopped.

'I can't do it,' he cried. 'I'm going back to bed.'

I asked him what the problem was, although I could guess.

'It was my daughter's wedding last night, so we were dancing and drinking until four o'clock in the morning. And the new Road Inspector is coming to visit today! He'll come and not find me, or he'll come and find me like this. Whatever happens, I'm finished.'

Then I had an idea. 'Does this new Inspector know you?'

'No. He started last week.'

'Where's your house?' He pointed to the small house I had seen before.

'Well, go back to bed,' I said, 'and sleep in peace. I'll do your job for the day and see the Inspector.'

He stared at me for a minute, then smiled.

'You're the man for me! It's an easy job.' He pointed to several big heaps of stones along the side of the road. 'Just put the stones down all along the edges of the road. My name's Alexander Turnbull, but my friends call me Ecky. If you speak to the Inspector politely, he'll be happy. I'll come back at five o'clock.'

I borrowed his glasses and a very dirty hat and gave him my good clothes. I also borrowed a very old pipe. My new friend walked off slowly to his bed. I hoped he would be inside his house when my enemies arrived.

I put as much dirt as possible on my face, hands and clothes, and rubbed some into my eyes to make them red. My boots did not look like a workman's boots, so I kicked them against the rocks to make them look older. The roadman had left his sandwiches and I was happy to eat some of them. There was still nothing moving on the road when I started work.

After some time I was getting hot, and I was beginning to count the hours until evening, when I heard a voice, and saw a young man in a small car looking at me.

'Are you Alexander Turnbull?' he said. 'I'm the new Road Inspector. You're doing these edges well, but there's a soft place about a kilometre down the hill. Don't forget that, will you? Good day now.'

Clearly, the Inspector thought I was the roadman. As time passed, one or two other cars came along the road, and I bought some biscuits from a travelling shop. Finally, a big car stopped and two men got out and walked towards me. I had seen them before – from the window of the hotel. The fatter of the two looked at me with sharp bright eyes.

'Good morning,' he said. 'That's an easy job you've got there.'

'There are worse jobs and there are better jobs,' I said. I spoke in Alexander Turnbull's strong Scottish accent.

The other man was looking at my boots. 'You've very fine boots. Were they made near here?'

'Oh no, they were made in London. I was given them by a man who was here on holiday last year.'

The fatter man spoke to the other in German. 'Let's move on. This man can't help us.'

They did ask one more question.

'Did you see anyone pass early this morning? Either on a bicycle or on foot?'

I pretended to think carefully.

'I wasn't up very early. You see, my daughter got married yesterday and I went to bed late. I looked out of the house at seven and there was nobody on the road. And I've seen no bicycles this morning.'

The thin man gave me a cigar, which I smelt and then put in my pocket. Then they got into the car and were soon out of sight.

I continued to work on the road, and I was right to do so. Ten minutes later they passed again, watching me carefully.

I hoped Mr Turnbull would stay in bed and I began to wonder what to do next. I couldn't mend roads for ever.

Just before five o'clock an open touring car came up the road, and stopped a few metres from me. The driver wanted to light a cigarette, and, by an extraordinary chance, I knew him. His name was Marmaduke Jopley and he was a man I disliked very much. He was only interested in people with money, and in visiting people who lived in beautiful houses in the country. I ran up to the car and took his arm.

'Hallo, Jopley.'

His mouth opened wide as he looked at me. 'Who are you?'

'My name's Hannay,' I said. 'You remember me.'

'The murderer!' he cried.

'Yes. And there'll be another murder if you don't help me. Give me your coat and hat.'

He did what I asked. He was very frightened. I put his coat and hat on, and put Mr Turnbull's hat on Jopley's head. I got in the car and started it.

'Now, my friend,' I said, 'you sit quietly and be a good boy. I'm going to borrow your car for an hour or two.'

I enjoyed the drive we had that evening. As we drove through the valley, I noticed some men beside the road, but

'*The murderer!*' Jopley cried.

they didn't look at us. I drove on into the hills and as it started to get dark, I turned up a small road and stopped in the middle of a lonely moor. I returned the hat and coat to Jopley.

'Thank you very much,' I said. 'You can be quite useful. Now you'd better go and find the police.'

As I sat on the moor and watched the car's lights disappear, I thought about my new life as a criminal. I was not a murderer, but I had developed a habit of stealing expensive cars.

6

THE BALD WRITER

I spent the night in the hills, in some thick heather behind a rock. I had no coat and I was very cold. My coat, Scudder's notebook, my watch and even my pipe and tobacco were with Mr Turnbull. All I had was some biscuits.

I had half the biscuits for supper and tried to keep warm in the heather. I was feeling quite pleased. So far I had been very lucky. The milkman, the man at the hotel, Sir Harry, the roadman and even Marmaduke had all helped me, and I felt that with help like this I might win. My main problem now was that I was very hungry. I fell asleep imagining the most beautiful meals.

I woke up very cold in the early morning. I looked down the hill, and in a second I was putting my boots on as fast as I could. There were men only a few hundred metres below me, walking up and searching the heather step by step.

Keeping low in the heather, I moved up the hill. At the top, I stood up and showed myself. I heard men shouting, and then I pretended to disappear over the top of the hill, but in fact I got down in the heather and crawled back down into the valley. After twenty minutes I looked back and saw the men disappearing over the top of the hill.

I didn't know where I was, but I knew I must keep moving. I was twenty minutes in front of them, but they were local men and they knew these hills better than I did. Soon they were close behind me and I was running as fast as I could. After a time I saw to my left some trees and the chimneys of a farmhouse. I ran down towards them and found myself in a garden. As I came nearer the house, I saw an old man looking at me through an open door. I crossed the garden and went in.

I was in a pleasant room, with books everywhere. At a desk in the middle sat an old man with a kind face. He had glasses on the end of his nose, and the top of his bald head shone like glass. He didn't move, but looked up and waited for me to speak.

I was so surprised by his calmness that for a minute I just stared at him.

'You're in a hurry, my friend,' he said slowly.

I looked out of the window at the moor. We could both see the line of men walking through the heather.

'Ah, I see,' he said. 'The police are after you, are they? Well, we'll talk about it later. I don't like the police in my house when I'm working. Go through that door on the left and close it behind you. You will be safe in there.'

And this extraordinary man picked up his pen and started to write.

I did what he said, and found myself in a small room with only a very small window high up in one wall. The door closed behind me. Once again I had found somewhere to hide.

But I didn't feel comfortable. There was something strange about the old man. I had suddenly appeared in his house, but he didn't seem surprised. And his eyes were frighteningly intelligent. I waited, and tried to forget that I was very hungry. I thought about breakfast, and suddenly the door opened and there was the old man again.

'I told the police you had gone over the hill. This is a lucky morning for you, Mr Richard Hannay,' he said, smiling.

As he spoke, his eyes half closed, and immediately I remembered Scudder's description of a man who could 'hood his eyes like a hawk'. I saw that I had walked into the hands of my enemies.

My first thought was to knock him down and run, but two men came through the door. They were carrying guns.

The old man knew my name, but he had never seen me before. I took a chance. 'I don't know what you mean,' I said roughly. 'And who are you calling Hannay? My name's Ainslie.'

'Of course, you have many names,' he said, still smiling. 'We won't argue about a name.'

I looked at him angrily. 'I suppose you're going to call the police back. I wish I'd never seen that car. Here's the money.' I put four pounds on the table.

'I won't call the police,' he said. 'This is a private problem between you and me.'

'Oh, stop it!' I cried. 'I've had no luck since I left my ship in Edinburgh. I found a crashed car and took a little money out of it, and I've had the police after me for two days. You do what you like. Ned Ainslie's finished.'

I could hear doubt in his voice when he next spoke.

'Would you be kind enough to tell me what you've been doing for the last few days?'

'I can't. I haven't eaten for two days. Give me something to eat and I'll tell you the truth.' I put on my best begging voice.

Some food was brought to me, and while I was eating, he said something to me in German. I stared at him stupidly. Then I told him my story. I was a sailor, and I had left my ship in Edinburgh to travel across Scotland to see my brother. I had found a car in a river and taken some money from it. But the police were now chasing me.

'They can have their money back,' I cried. 'It's only brought me trouble!'

'You're good at lying, Hannay,' he said.

I started to get very angry. 'My name's Ainslie and I don't know anybody called Hannay. I'd rather have the police than you and your guns and your Hannays. No, I'm sorry, sir, I'm grateful for the food, but I'd like to go now.'

I could see that he was not sure. He had never seen me, and I suppose I did not look like my photograph.

'I won't let you go. If you are Mr Ainslie, then you'll soon be able to prove it. If you're not, then I have a surprise for you.'

I had walked into the hands of my enemies.

He rang a bell, and a third servant appeared.

'I want the car in five minutes,' he said. 'There will be three for lunch.'

Then he looked at me, and that was the most frightening thing of all. His eyes were unnatural – bright, cold and evil. I tried to stare back, and even to smile.

'You'll know me next time we meet,' I said.

'Karl,' he said, speaking in German. 'Put this man in the back room until I return.'

I was taken out of the room with a gun at each ear.

* * *

The back room was very dark and full of old bottles and boxes. The windows had shutters on the outside. The key turned in the door, and I could hear the feet of the guards outside.

I sat down feeling very unhappy. The old man had gone to collect his friends, the men who had talked to me when I was the roadman. They would soon discover that I was not the roadman, nor Mr Ainslie, but Richard Hannay. I began to wish I had been found by the police; I would feel safer with them than with this man and his two friends.

They were coming for lunch, so I had only two hours. I tried the windows but they would not move. I felt the boxes and bottles, and then found a door in the wall. It was a cupboard door, and it was locked. I had nothing else to do so I pulled on it until it opened.

There were a lot of things inside. On one shelf there were some matches, and I used them to look more closely. At the back of one shelf was a strong wooden box. I broke it open and found, to my surprise, some fuses and several small square packets of explosive.

I knew that with these I could blow the house up. The problem was that I didn't know how much to use. If I used too much, I would blow myself up. But if I didn't use them at all, I would be dead in three hours.

I put one of the squares of explosive near the door, and put a fuse from there to the other side of the room. I lit the fuse and hid behind some boxes. There was silence for five seconds . . .

The wall exploded into a bright yellow light, something fell on my left arm, and I became unconscious.

I was unconscious for only a few seconds. Then I stood up, trying not to breathe the yellow smoke. The window had been blown out and I climbed out into the garden. Across the garden there were some buildings, and one was an old tower. I felt too ill to go very far, and that seemed the best hiding place.

The climb up the outside of that tower was the most difficult thing I ever did. My head felt terrible, and the smoke had made me very sick, but in the end I managed it, and lay down at the top. Then I became unconscious again.

When I woke up, my head was burning and the sun was shining into my face. I lay for a long time without moving. I could hear men talking. I looked through a hole in the wall and saw men with guns. There was the bald man and I thought I could see the fat one too.

For half an hour they searched all the buildings. They came to the door at the bottom of my tower, and for a minute I thought they were going to come up, but the door was locked.

All afternoon I lay on that roof. I was terribly thirsty, and, to make it worse, I could see and hear a small stream which came off the moor and flowed near the farm. I wanted a drink of that cool clear water more than anything in the world.

From the tower I could see all the moor around. I saw two men go off in a car, and another man on a horse, and I imagined they were looking for me. But I could also see something more interesting. At the top of the hill behind the house was a ring of trees with grass inside. It was clear that this was where the plane landed.

It was an excellent place for an airfield. It could not be seen from below because it was at the top of the hill; from the valley, the hill seemed covered with trees. And anyone watching the plane coming in to land would think it was just flying over the hill. I realized that if the plane arrived now, the pilot would probably see me, so I lay still, and hoped night would come quickly.

Luckily, when the plane did arrive, it was almost dark. I watched it land, and then waited until everything was quiet. There was no moon, and I was too thirsty to wait, so at nine o'clock I climbed down. Halfway down, somebody came out of the house with a light, and I froze. Then the light disappeared and I continued down to the ground.

I crawled as far as the trees. I guessed that the house would be guarded in some way, so I continued very slowly and carefully, and found a wire about sixty centimetres from the ground. Falling over that would doubtless start alarm bells ringing in the house.

A hundred metres further on there was another wire, but

The climb up the tower was the most difficult thing I ever did.

after that it was the open moor. Ten minutes later I had my head in the stream and I drank litres of cold water.

I did not stop again until I was ten kilometres from that terrible house.

7

THE FISHERMAN

I sat on a hill-top and thought about my next move. I wasn't very happy, because although I had escaped, I was feeling very ill. The smoke had been very unpleasant, and the day on the roof had made things worse. I had a terrible headache, and my arm hurt so badly that I could not move it.

I decided to go back to Mr Turnbull's house and find my clothes and Scudder's notebook. Then I would take a train to the south. The sooner I met Sir Harry's friend in the government, Sir Walter Bullivant, the better. I hoped he would believe my story, but, even if he did not, I would be safer with him, or even the British police, than with those men at the farmhouse.

It was a clear, starry night and easy to find my way across the hills. I thought I was probably about thirty kilometres from Mr Turnbull's house, so I could not get there in one night. I would have to hide somewhere for the day. When it started to get light, I stopped to wash in a river and then knocked on the door of a small house. I told the woman who lived there that I had had a bad fall, and she could see that I was not well. She gave me some milk and whisky. She also gave me an old coat and hat of her husband's. I now looked like every other Scotsman, and felt safer.

It started to rain, and I spent the afternoon under a rock. That night was the most miserable of all. There were no stars, and I got lost at least twice. I had about fifteen kilometres more to go, but I think I walked thirty. In the end, in the very early morning, in a thick fog, I knocked on Mr Turnbull's door.

Mr Turnbull opened the door wearing an old black suit and a tie. At first he did not recognize me.

'What are you doing here at this time on a Sunday morning?'

My head was so bad that I could not answer for a moment, but then he recognized me, and saw that I was ill.

'Have you got my glasses?' he asked.

I took them out of my pocket and gave them to him.

'You want your clothes,' he said. 'Come in. You're not looking well at all. Come and sit down.'

I realized that my malaria had come back. I had had malaria in Africa, and it returned sometimes. The smoke, my arm, the wet and the cold had probably not helped. Soon, Mr Turnbull was helping me into a bed.

He was a good friend, that roadman. He took care of me for ten days, until my fever had gone and my arm was much better. He went out to work every day, locking the door, and in the evening he sat by the fire. He asked no questions, but on some days he brought me a newspaper, and I saw that the excitement over the Langham Place murder was over.

One day he gave me my money back. 'There's a lot of money there. You'd better count it and see if it's all there.'

I wanted to move as soon as possible, but it was not until the 12th of June that I felt well enough to go. I made Turnbull accept some money for my food, but it was difficult.

I walked the twenty kilometres to the station in a day. The train to London did not leave until night, so I rested in the heather until it arrived. I was very happy to be in the train, and on the way south.

* * *

I slept on the train until early morning. Then I changed trains two or three times. At about eight o'clock in the evening I arrived at the small station at Artinswell, to the west of London. The road led through a wood into a green valley. Soon I came to a bridge and looked down into the river, whistling the song 'Annie Làurie'.

A fisherman walked up from the river, and as he got near to me, he started to whistle the same song. He was a big man in old clothes and a wide hat. He smiled at me, and I looked at his kind, intelligent face.

'The water's clear, isn't it?' he said. 'Look at that big fish lying on the bottom. I've been trying to catch him all evening.'

'I can't see him,' I said.

'Look, over there, near those plants.'

'Oh yes, I can see him now. He looks like a black stone.'

He whistled again, then paused. 'Your name's Twisdon, isn't it?'

'No,' I said. 'I mean yes.' I had forgotten the name I had

given Sir Harry.

'It's a good idea to know your own name,' he said, smiling.

I looked at him again and began to think that this kind, intelligent man would be a real ally at last.

Then he pointed to a house by the river and said quietly, 'Wait five minutes, then come to the back door.' He walked off.

I did as he asked, and found the back door open and a servant waiting.

'Come this way, sir,' he said, and took me to a bedroom. There were clothes waiting for me, and shaving things. 'There's a bathroom next door. Dinner is in half an hour.'

The servant left, and I sat down. I was very surprised, but also delighted. Sir Walter clearly believed that I was not a murderer, although when I looked at myself in the mirror, I thought I looked very much like one.

I had a bath and shaved and put on the clothes. When I had finished, I looked in the mirror again. This time I saw a completely different young man.

Sir Walter was waiting for me in the dining room. I decided I must tell him the truth about myself immediately.

'I must thank you very much, but I must make something clear,' I said. 'I'm not a murderer, but the police want me. If you'd like me to leave, I'll leave now.'

He smiled. 'That's all right. We won't let it stop us eating. Let's talk after dinner.'

The food and wine were excellent. After dinner we went to the sitting-room for coffee and he looked at me.

'I've done what Harry asked me to do,' he said. 'He told

me you'd tell me a story to wake me up if I did. So what is
your story, Mr Hannay?'

I noticed that he was using my real name.

I told him the whole story, from the night I came home
and found Scudder at my door. I told him what Scudder
had told me about Karolides, and saw him smile once or
twice. Then I told him about the murder, and the milkman,
and Scotland, and Scudder's notebook.

'You've got it here?' he asked, and looked pleased when
I took it from my pocket.

I said nothing about what I had read in Scudder's notes.
Then I told him about my meeting with Sir Harry, and he
laughed. My day as a roadman interested him. He made me
describe the two men in the car, and seemed to be thinking
hard. Then he laughed again at my adventure with
Marmaduke Jopley. When I described the old man in the
farmhouse, he stopped smiling.

'Old, bald, and hoods his eyes like a hawk. I don't like
the sound of him. And you blew up his house. You're a
brave man.'

I reached the end of my story. He stood up, by the fire,
and looked down at me.

'You don't need to worry about the police,' he said.
'They don't want you any more.'

'Have they arrested the murderer?'

'No. But they know it's not you.'

'How?'

'Because I heard from Scudder. I knew him a bit. He was
a strange man, but he was honest. I had a letter from him on
the 31st of May.'

'But he'd been dead for a week by then.'

'The letter was written and posted on the 23rd. His letters usually went to Spain and then Newcastle, so they took a week to arrive.'

'What did he say?'

'That he was in danger. He said he was living in Langham Place, and that he was with a good friend. I think he wanted to help you in case he was murdered. When I got the letter, I went to Scotland Yard and talked to the police.'

You can imagine that I felt ten times better. I was a free man, and my only enemies were my country's enemies.

'Now, let's see this notebook,' said Sir Walter.

It took us an hour to work through it. I explained the code and he understood very quickly. When we had finished, he sat silent for a while.

'I don't understand all of this,' he said at last. 'He's right about one thing, and that is the meeting on the 15th. How can anyone have discovered about that? But all this about war and the Black Stone – it's very strange. Scudder did like to make things seem important and exciting.

'The Black Stone,' he repeated. 'It's like a cheap detective story. And all this about Karolides can't be true. Karolides will be alive when we're both dead. No, Scudder's wrong there. There are some unpleasant things going on. Scudder found something out and got killed for it. But all this about stealing the Navy's war plans . . . I can't really believe it.'

Just then, the servant came into the room.

'There's a telephone call from London for you, sir.'

Sir Walter went out. He came back five minutes later with a white face. 'I apologize to Scudder,' he whispered,

'Karolides was shot dead at seven o'clock this evening.'

and then looked at me. 'Karolides was shot dead at seven o'clock this evening.'

8

THE COMING OF THE BLACK STONE

I came down to breakfast the next morning and found Sir Walter reading a coded message. He seemed less relaxed than yesterday.

'I was very busy for an hour after you went to bed,' he said. 'I've arranged for the Frenchman, Royer, to come a day early. He will be in London at five o'clock. I don't think the change of day will help very much. If our enemies already knew he was coming, they will probably find out that the plans have changed. I would love to know how the news of his visit escaped.'

While I ate, he continued to talk. I was surprised that he was telling me all these important secrets.

'Can't the Navy's war plans be changed?' I asked.

'They could,' he said. 'But we want to avoid that. It would be very difficult, and some changes would be impossible. But the big problem is that they're not going to steal the plans in the street. They'll try to get the details without anybody knowing, and Royer will return to Paris thinking that everything is still secret.'

'Then we must stay at Royer's side until he is home again,' I said.

'Royer will meet us after dinner at my house in London: there'll be Whittaker from the Navy, myself, Sir Arthur Drew, and General Winstanley. The First Sea Lord, the head of the Navy, has been ill, and may not be able to come. Whittaker will give Royer the important papers, and then Royer will be driven to Portsmouth where a Navy ship will take him to France. He will be watched until he is back there. Whittaker will be watched while he has the papers before he meets Royer. It's the best we can do, and I don't see what can go wrong. But I'm very nervous because of the murder of Karolides.'

After breakfast he asked me to be his driver for the day.

'You know what these people are like, and I don't want to take risks.'

In London we went first to Scotland Yard where we met an important-looking policeman.

'I've brought you the Langham Place murderer,' said Sir Walter.

The policeman smiled. 'I wish you had. I imagine you are Mr Hannay. We were very interested in you for a few days.'

'Mr Hannay will interest you again, MacGillivray, but his story must wait twenty-four hours. But I would like you to tell Mr Hannay that you don't want to arrest him any more.'

'Of course we don't.' The policeman turned to me. 'Your flat and your servant are waiting for you, although you may not want to return there.'

As Sir Walter and I left, he said I was free for the rest of the day. 'Come and see me tomorrow, Hannay. I don't need to tell you to keep everything secret. You had better stay out of sight. If your Black Stone friends see you, there might be trouble.'

* * *

I didn't know what to do. It was strange to be a free man. I went to a very good restaurant for lunch, but I was still feeling nervous. When anybody looked at me, I wondered if they were thinking about the murder. I walked around London, thinking. I knew that by now Royer would be in England, and I felt sure that something terrible was going to happen and that only I could stop it. But it was not my business now.

I didn't want to go back to my flat. I had to go back some

time, but I decided to stay at a hotel tonight.

I had supper in another restaurant, and thought that after that I would go to Sir Walter's house. He might not want me there, but I would feel happier if I went.

As I walked through London towards his house, I met a group of young men. One of them was Marmaduke Jopley.

'It's the murderer!' he cried. 'Stop him! That's Hannay, the Langham Place murderer!' He took hold of my arm, and the others crowded round me.

I didn't want trouble, but I was feeling angry. A policeman came up, and instead of explaining the mistake to him quietly and sensibly, I just hit out wildly at Marmaduke's stupid face. I felt much happier when he was lying on his back in the road. Then a general fight started, until the policeman got hold of me. I heard him ask what the matter was, and Marmaduke, talking through his broken teeth, told him that I was Hannay the murderer.

I was so angry that I pushed the policeman one way and one of Marmaduke's friends the other, and ran as fast as I could. There was shouting behind me, but I had escaped. I ran all the way to Sir Walter's house, walked up to the door and rang. I hoped the door would open quickly.

It did.

'I must see Sir Walter,' I said to the servant. 'It's desperately important.'

The servant let me in, and then shut the door behind me. 'Sir Walter is in a meeting, sir. Perhaps you will wait.'

There was a telephone and one or two chairs in the hall, and I sat down there.

'Listen,' I whispered to the servant. 'I'm in a bit of

trouble, but I'm working for Sir Walter. If anyone comes to the door and asks for me, tell them I'm not here.'

There was a sudden ringing at the door, and he went to open it. He told them whose house it was, and that nobody could come in, and then shut the door.

* * *

A few minutes later there was another ring at the door, and the servant did not hesitate to let this visitor in. Everybody knew his face from the newspapers – a square, grey beard and bright blue eyes. Lord Alloa, the First Sea Lord, and head of the British Navy.

He was shown into a room at the end of the hall. I sat there for twenty minutes. Surely the meeting would end soon; Royer must leave for Portsmouth by eleven o'clock.

Then the door opened again and the First Sea Lord came out. He walked past me, and in passing he looked at me and for a second I looked into his eyes It was only for a second, but my heart jumped. The First Sea Lord had never seen me before, but in his eyes I saw that he recognized me. Then he passed me and was out of the door into the street.

I picked up the telephone book and looked up the number of Lord Alloa's house. I spoke to one of his servants.

'Is Lord Alloa at home?' I asked.

'Yes, but he's ill and has been in bed all day. Do you want to leave a message, sir?'

I put down the telephone and sat down, shaking. My part in this business was not finished. I walked straight into the room where the others were meeting.

Sir Walter looked surprised and annoyed. 'I'm afraid

*The First Sea Lord had never seen me before,
but I saw that he recognized me.*

that this is not a good time, Mr Hannay.'

'I think it is,' I answered. 'Tell me, please, who left this
room a minute ago.'

'Lord Alloa,' said Sir Walter, looking angrier.

'It was not,' I cried. 'It looked like him but it was not him.
It was a man who recognized me, who has seen me in the

last month. I've just telephoned Lord Alloa's house and
he's been ill in bed all day.'

'Who . . .' someone asked.

'The Black Stone,' I cried, sitting down, and looking at
five frightened men.

9

THE THIRTY-NINE STEPS

Sir Walter got up and left the room. He came back after ten
minutes. 'I've spoken to Alloa. I got him out of bed – he was
very angry. He hasn't left his house all day.'

'It's impossible,' said Winstanley. 'I sat next to him for
nearly half an hour.'

'That's what's so clever,' I said. 'You were too interested
in other things to look at him closely. You knew that he
might be well enough to come tonight and, as First Sea
Lord, it was natural for him to be here. Why should you
suspect that it wasn't him?'

Then the Frenchman spoke, very slowly, and in good
English.

'This young man is right. He understands our enemies.
People only see what they expect to see. This man came
late, spoke little, and left early – but he behaved exactly as
we would expect Lord Alloa to behave.'

'But I don't understand,' said Winstanley. 'Our enemies
don't want us to know what they have learnt about our war
plans. But if one of us talked to Alloa about tonight's

meeting, we would discover immediately that he hadn't been here.'

Sir Walter laughed angrily. 'That shows their cleverness again, in choosing Alloa. They took a risk, but everybody knows that Alloa is a sick man and is often too ill to go to meetings. And even when he is well, he is impatient, difficult, and a man of very few words. Which of us was likely to speak to him about tonight?'

'But the spy hasn't taken the plans,' said Winstanley. 'He saw them, but could he carry away pages of information in his head?'

'It's not difficult,' said the Frenchman. 'A good spy can remember things photographically.'

'Well, I suppose we'll have to change our plans,' said Sir Walter unhappily.

'There's another problem,' said Royer. 'I said a lot about the plans of the French army. That information will be very valuable to our enemies. That man, and his friends, must be stopped immediately.'

'They could simply send their information in a letter,' said Whittaker. 'It may already be in the post.'

'No,' said Royer. 'A spy brings home his information personally and he collects his pay personally. These men must cross the sea, so we still have a chance. You must watch the coast and search ships. It is desperately important for both France and Britain.'

Royer was right. We could do something. But none of us felt very hopeful. How, among the forty million people in Britain, could we find the three cleverest criminals in Europe?

* * *

Then, suddenly, I had an idea.

'Where is Scudder's book?' I asked Sir Walter. 'Quick, I remember something in it.'

He gave it to me.

I found the place. 'Thirty-nine steps,' I read, and again, 'Thirty-nine steps – I counted them – high tide, 10.17 p.m.'

Whittaker clearly thought I had gone mad.

'Don't you see it's a clue?' I cried. 'Scudder knew where they were going to leave England. Tomorrow was the day, and it's somewhere where high tide is at 10.17.'

'Perhaps they've already gone tonight,' someone suggested.

'Not them. They have their own secret way, and why should they hurry? They don't know that we're after them. Where can I get a book of Tide Tables?'

Whittaker looked happier. 'It's a chance,' he said. 'Let's go to the Navy Offices.'

Sir Walter went off to Scotland Yard to get MacGillivray. The rest of us drove to the Navy Offices where we went to a big room full of books and maps. We got a copy of the Tide Tables, and I sat down and looked through it while the others watched.

It was no good. There were more than fifty places where high tide was at 10.17. We needed more information than that.

I thought hard. What did Scudder mean by steps, and why was it so important to count them? It must be somewhere with several paths going down to the sea. This path would be the only one with thirty-nine steps.

I had another thought and checked the time of regular ships leaving England. There was no ship at 10.17.

Why was high tide important? In a big harbour the tide doesn't matter. It is only important in a small harbour, or somewhere where there is no harbour at all.

Then I thought about where a man would leave England if he were going to Germany. Not from the south coast, or the west coast, or Scotland. It would be somewhere on the east coast, probably between Cromer and Dover.

I am not Sherlock Holmes. But I am used to using my head, and when I guess, my guesses are often right.

I wrote out my ideas on a piece of paper:

ALMOST CERTAIN

(1) A place where there are several paths down to the sea. One of these has thirty-nine steps.

(2) High tide at 10.17 p.m. A place where it is only possible for a ship to leave the coast at high tide.

(3) Probably not a harbour, but open coast with cliffs and a beach.

(4) Ship probably a small one, a yacht or a fishing boat.

(5) Somewhere on the east coast between Cromer and Dover.

It seemed strange to be sitting at a table, watched by a group of very important people, trying to understand something written by a dead man. But it was a matter of life or death to us.

Sir Walter and MacGillivray arrived. They had men watching all the harbours and railway stations with descriptions of the three men. But none of us thought that

It was a matter of life and death to us.

this would help.

'Here's the best I can do,' I said. 'We have to find a place where there is a path with thirty-nine steps down to a beach. It must be somewhere on the east coast. Of course, it's somewhere where high tide is at 10.17 tomorrow night. Who can we ask who knows the east coast really well?'

Whittaker said he knew a man who lived in south London. He went off in a car to get him and came back at about one o'clock in the morning with an old sailor who had worked all his life on the east coast.

'We want you to tell us about places you know on the east coast where there are cliffs and steps going down to the beach,' said Winstanley.

He thought for a minute or two. 'There are a lot of seaside towns – holiday places – where there are steps from the town down to the beach.'

'No, that's not private enough,' I said.

'Well, I don't know. Of course, there's the Ruff—'

'What's that?'

'It's in Kent, near Bradgate. There are cliffs with houses along the top – big houses. Some of the houses have steps down to a beach. Mostly rich people live there, the sort of people who like to be private.'

I opened the Tide Tables at Bradgate. High tide was at 10.27 on the 15th of June.

'This looks hopeful,' I cried. 'How can I find out when high tide is at the Ruff?'

'I can tell you that, sir,' said the sailor. 'I used to go fishing there. High tide is ten minutes before Bradgate.'

I closed the book and looked up at the others.

'If one of those paths has thirty-nine steps, then I think we have a good chance,' I said. 'Can I take a car, Sir Walter, and a map? If Mr MacGillivray can help me, perhaps we can prepare something for tomorrow.'

It seemed strange for me to take control like this. But I was used to action, and they could see it. It was the Frenchman, Royer, who said what they were all thinking. 'I am quite happy,' he said, 'to leave this business in Mr Hannay's hands.'

At half-past three in the morning I was driving through Kent in the moonlight, with MacGillivray next to me.

MEETINGS BY THE SEA

It was a fine, blue June morning, and I was outside a hotel in Bradgate looking out to sea. There was a ship out there, and I could see that it was a warship of some kind. MacGillivray had been in the navy and knew the ship. I sent a message to Sir Walter to ask if it could help us if necessary.

After breakfast we walked along the beach under the Ruff. I kept hidden, while MacGillivray counted the six lots of steps in the cliff.

I waited for an hour while he counted, and when I saw him coming towards me with a piece of paper, I was very nervous.

He read out the numbers. 'Thirty-four, thirty-five, thirty-nine, forty-two, forty-seven, and twenty-one.' I almost got up and shouted.

We walked back to Bradgate quickly. MacGillivray had six policemen sent down from London. He then went off to look at the house at the top of the thirty-nine steps.

The information he brought back was neither good nor bad. The house was called Trafalgar House, and belonged to an old man called Appleton. He was there at the moment. The neighbours didn't know him well. MacGillivray had then gone to the back door of the house, pretending to be a man selling sewing machines. There were three servants, and he spoke to the cook. He was sure she knew nothing. Next door a new house was being built, which might be a good place to watch from; and on the other side the house was empty. Its garden was rather wild, and would also be a good place to hide in.

I took a telescope and found a good hiding place from which to watch the house. I watched for a time, and saw an old man leave the house and walk into the back garden at the top of the cliff. He sat down to read a newspaper, but he looked out to sea several times. I thought he was probably looking at the warship. I watched him for half an hour, until he went back into the house for lunch. Then I went back to the hotel for mine.

I wasn't feeling very confident. That old man might be the old man I had met in the farmhouse on the moors. But there are hundreds of old men in houses by the sea, and he was probably just a nice old man on his holidays.

After lunch I sat in front of the hotel and looked out to sea; and then I felt happier, because I saw something new. A yacht came up the coast and stopped a few hundred metres off the Ruff. MacGillivray and I went down to the harbour, got a boat, and spent the afternoon fishing.

We caught quite a lot of fish, and then, at about four o'clock, went to look at the yacht. It looked like a fast boat and its name was the *Ariadne*. I spoke to a sailor who was cleaning the side of the boat, and he was certainly English. So was the next sailor we spoke to, and we had quite a long conversation about the weather.

Then, suddenly, the men stopped talking and started work again, and a man in uniform walked up. He was a pleasant, friendly man, and asked us about the fishing in very good English. But I was sure that he was not English himself.

I felt a little more confident after seeing him, but as we went back to Bradgate, I was still not sure. My enemies had killed Scudder because they thought he was a danger to them. They had tried to kill me – for the same reason. So why hadn't they changed their escape plans? They didn't know about Scudder's black notebook, but why stay with the same plan when there was a chance that I knew about it? It seemed a stupid risk to take.

I decided to spend an hour or two watching Trafalgar House and found a good place where I could look down on the garden. I could see two men playing tennis. One was the

At about four o'clock we went to look at the yacht.

old man I had already seen; the other was a younger, fatter man. They played well, and were clearly enjoying themselves like two businessmen on holiday. I have never seen anything more harmless. They stopped for a drink, and I asked myself if I wasn't the most stupid man alive. These were two normal, boring Englishmen, not the clever murderers that I had met in Scotland.

Then a third man arrived on a bicycle. He walked into the garden and started talking to the tennis players. They were all laughing in a very English way. Soon they went back into the house, laughing and talking, and I stayed there feeling stupid. These men might be acting, but why? They didn't know I was watching and listening to them. They were just three perfectly normal, harmless Englishmen.

* * *

But there were three of them: and one was old, and one was fat, and one was thin and dark. And a yacht was waiting a kilometre away with at least one German on it. I thought about Karolides lying dead, and all Europe trembling on the edge of war, and about the men waiting in London, hoping that I would do something to stop these spies.

I decided there was only one thing to do. I had to continue and just hope for the best. I didn't want to do it. I would rather walk into a room full of wild animals than walk into that happy English house and tell those three men they were under arrest. How they would laugh at me!

Then I remembered something that an old friend in Africa once told me. He had often been in trouble with the police. He once talked about disguises with me, and he said that the way somebody looked was not the real secret. He said that what mattered was the 'feel' of somebody. If you moved to completely different surroundings, and if you looked comfortable and at home there, you would be very difficult to recognize. My friend had once borrowed a black coat and tie and gone to church and stood next to the policeman who was looking for him. The policeman had only seen him shooting out the lights in a pub, and he did not recognize him in a church.

Perhaps these people were playing the same game. A stupid man tries to look different; a clever man looks the same and *is* different.

My friend had also told me this: 'If you want to disguise yourself, you must believe that you're the person you're pretending to be.' That would explain the game of tennis. These men weren't acting; they just changed from one life to another, and the new life was as natural as the old. It is the secret of all great criminals.

It was now about eight o'clock. I went back to see MacGillivray and we arranged where the other policemen would hide. After that I went for a walk along the coast, looking at the peaceful people on holiday. Out at sea I could see lights on the *Ariadne*, and on the warship, and, further away, the lights of other ships. Everything seemed so normal and peaceful that I couldn't believe the three men were my criminals. But I turned and walked towards Trafalgar House at about half past nine.

MacGillivray's men were, I supposed, in their hiding places. The house was quiet, but I could just hear the sound of voices; the men were just finishing their dinner. Feeling very stupid, I walked up to the door and rang the bell.

When a servant opened the door, I asked for Mr Appleton and was shown in. I had planned to walk straight in and surprise the men into recognizing me. But I started looking at all the pictures on the wall. There were photographs of groups of English schoolboys and lots of other things that you only find in an English home. The servant walked in front of me into the dining-room and told the men who I was, and I missed the chance of surprise.

When I walked in, the old man stood up and turned round to meet me. The other two turned to look at me. The old man was perfectly polite.

'Mr Hannay?' he said. 'Did you wish to see me?'

I pulled up a chair and sat down.

'I think we've met before,' I said, 'and I guess you know why I'm here.'

The light in the room was not bright, but I think they all looked very surprised.

'Perhaps, perhaps,' said the old man. 'I'm afraid I don't remember faces very well. You'll have to tell me why you're here, because I really don't know.'

'Well,' I said, although I didn't really believe what I was saying, 'I have come to arrest all three of you.'

'Arrest!' said the old man in surprise. 'Arrest! What for?'

'For the murder of Franklin Scudder in London on the 23rd of May.'

'I've never heard the name before,' said the old man.

One of the others spoke. 'That was the Langham Place murder. I read about that in the newspapers. But you must be mad! Where do you come from?'

'Scotland Yard,' I said.

Then there was silence for a moment until the fat one started to talk, hesitating a lot between words.

'Don't worry, uncle. It's all a stupid mistake. Even the police make mistakes. I wasn't even in England on the 23rd, and Bob was in hospital. You were in London, but you can explain what you were doing.'

'You're right, Percy, it's easy. The 23rd! That was the day after Agatha's wedding. Yes, I had lunch with Charlie Symons and in the evening I went to the Cardwells'. Why, they gave me that!' He pointed to a cigar box on the table.

'I think you will see that you have made a mistake,' the thin dark man said to me politely. 'We are quite happy to help Scotland Yard, and we don't want the police to make stupid mistakes. That's so, isn't it, uncle?'

'Certainly, Bob.' The old man looked happier now. 'Certainly we'll help if we can. But this is madness.'

'This will make our friends laugh,' said the fat man. 'They think we're boring and that nothing ever happens to us.' He began to laugh very pleasantly.

'Yes, it's a good story. Really, Mr Hannay, I should be angry, but it's too funny. You really frightened me! You looked so serious. I thought I'd killed somebody in my sleep!'

They weren't acting. There was nothing false about them. At first I wanted to apologize and leave. Then I stood up and went to the door and turned on the main light. I looked at the three faces.

I saw nothing to help me. One was old and bald, one was fat, one was dark and thin. They could be the three men I had seen in Scotland, but I could see nothing to prove it.

'Well,' said the old man politely, 'are you sure now that we are not murderers, or are you going to take us to the police station?'

There was nothing to do except call in the men outside and arrest them, or say I had made a mistake and leave. And I couldn't decide.

'While we're waiting, let's have a game of cards,' said the fat one. 'It will give Mr Hannay time to think, and we need a fourth player. Will you play?'

I agreed, but everything suddenly seemed unreal. We went into another room, where there was a table and cards. The window was open and the moon was shining on the cliffs and the sea. We played and they talked. I'm usually quite good at cards, but that night I played extremely badly.

* * *

Then something woke me up.

The old man put his cards down for a moment and sat back in his chair with his hand on his knee. It was a movement I had seen before, in that farm on the moors, with two servants with guns behind me. Suddenly my head cleared and I looked at the three men differently.

It was ten o'clock.

The three faces seemed to change in front of my eyes. The thin dark man was the murderer. His knife had killed Scudder. The fat man had been the First Sea Lord last night.

But the old man was the worst. How had I ever thought he looked kind and friendly? His eyes were cold and evil and frightening. I went on playing, but I hated him more and more with every card.

'Look at the time, Bob,' said the old man. 'Don't forget you've got a train to catch. He must be in London tonight,' he said, turning to me. His voice now sounded completely false.

'I'm afraid he must wait,' I said.

'Oh, no!' said the thin man. 'I thought you'd finished with that. I must go. You can have my address.'

'No,' I said, 'you must stay.'

I think then they realized they were in real trouble. I looked at the old man and I saw his eyes hood like a hawk.

I blew my whistle.

Immediately the lights went out. Someone held me to my chair.

'Quickly, Franz,' somebody shouted in German, 'the boat, the boat!' I saw two policemen on the grass behind the house.

The thin dark man jumped through the window and was across the grass before anybody could stop him. I was fighting the old man, and more police came into the room. I saw them holding the fat man. But the thin man was at the top of the steps. I waited, holding the old man, for the time it would take the thin man to get to the sea.

Suddenly, the old man escaped from me and ran to the wall of the room. From underneath the ground I heard an explosion. The cliff and the steps had been blown up.

The old man looked at me with wild, crazy eyes.

'He is safe,' he cried. 'You cannot follow him. The Black Stone has won.'

This old man was more than just a paid spy. Those hooded eyes shone with a deep, burning love for his

The thin dark man jumped through the window.

country. But as the police took him away, I had one more
thing to say.

'Your friend has not won. We put our men on the
Ariadne an hour ago.'

* * *

Seven weeks later, as all the world knows, we went to war.
I joined the army in the first week. But I did my best work,
I think, before I put on uniform.

GLOSSARY

ally a person or country that has an agreement with another or gives help

biscuit a kind of thin, dry cake, usually small and round

candidate a person who is trying to win an election

carriage one part of a train

clue a thing, or a piece of information, that helps to find the answer to a problem or a crime

code secret writing, using letters or numbers

crawl to move slowly with your body close to the ground

direction the line along which a person looks or moves

disguise *(v)* to make yourself look different so that people don't recognize you

election a time when people vote to choose a new government

evidence things which show whether something is true or not

evil very bad

explosive *(n)* something that can explode

fuse a long string which is used to light an explosive

government the group of people who control a country

harbour a place where ships can stop safely next to the land

hawk a bird which kills and eats small animals and birds

heap a lot of things, one on top of the other

heather a short plant with purple flowers which grows on moors

hedge a thick line of low trees and bushes

hood *(v)* (in this story) to half-close your eyes

lisp *(v and n)* to speak in a way that makes an 's' sound like 'th'

malaria a disease carried by an insect, which gives a high fever

milkman a man who takes milk to houses every morning

moor open, rough land on hills with no trees

navy all the warships of one country

nervous afraid, not confident

officer an important person in an army

path a small road for people to walk on

point *(v)* to show with your hand where something is

politics the life, work, and business of government

Prime Minister the leader of a government

relaxed feeling calm and peaceful, not excited or worried

risk *(n)* a chance that could bring danger

rude not polite

Scotland Yard the headquarters of the police in London

servant a person who is paid to cook and clean for another
person

shave to cut the hair off a man's face

shutter a wooden or metal door outside a window

stream a small river

submarine a ship that can travel under the water

telescope a long tube for seeing things which are a long way
away

tide the rise and fall of the sea every twelve hours

timetable a list which gives the times of trains

tobacco jar a special box for the tobacco smoked in a pipe

tower a tall, narrow building

trust to believe that somebody is honest

whistle *(v)* to make a high clear sound by blowing through a
small hole between partly closed lips

wine an alcoholic drink made from grapes

wire a long thin piece of metal, like a string

yacht a sailing boat

The Thirty-Nine Steps

ACTIVITIES

ACTIVITIES

Before Reading

1 Read the back cover and the story introduction on the first page of the book. Are these sentences true (T) or false (F)?

1 Richard Hannay has killed a man.

2 Hannay has run away to Scotland.

3 The 'Black Stone' is the name of a famous policeman.

4 Hannay has got a notebook that belonged to a dead man.

2 What is going to happen in the story? Can you guess? For each sentence, circle Y (Yes) or N (No).

1 Hannay will go back to Africa. Y/N

2 The people in the plane will see Hannay. Y/N

3 The 'Black Stone' will kill Hannay. Y/N

4 The police will catch Hannay and put him in prison. Y/N

5 Someone will be murdered in London in June. Y/N

6 Hannay will catch Scudder's murderer. Y/N

3 The 'thirty-nine steps' are important in the story. Where do you think they are? Choose one of these answers.

1 in a castle in Scotland

2 beside the sea in England

3 in an office building in London

4 on a mountain in Africa

ACTIVITIES

While Reading

Read Chapters 1 and 2, and then answer these questions.

1 How long had Hannay been away from Britain?
2 How did he feel after three months in Britain?
3 Why did he stop feeling bored?
4 What did Scudder say was going to happen on 15th June?
5 How did Scudder die?
6 Why didn't Hannay call the police when he found Scudder's body?
7 Where did he decide to go?
8 How did he disguise himself?

Read Chapters 3 and 4. Are these sentences true (T) or false (F)? Rewrite the false ones with the correct information.

1 The writing in Scudder's notebook was mostly words.
2 Hannay took the train from Dumfries to Galloway and then travelled back towards Dumfries.
3 The hotel owner thought that Hannay's story was terrible.
4 The key to Scudder's code was the name Julia Czechenyi.
5 Hannay stole the car that belonged to the police.
6 Hannay spoke about Africa at the election meeting.
7 Hannay told Sir Harry the whole story.
8 Sir Harry wrote a letter to his uncle.

Before you read Chapter 5, can you guess what happens? For each sentence, circle Y (Yes) or N (No).

1 The plane comes back to look for Hannay. Y/N
2 Hannay leaves the bicycle in the middle of the road. Y/N
3 Hannay disguises himself again. Y/N
4 Hannay meets a man that he knows. Y/N
5 Hannay steals another car. Y/N

Read Chapters 5 and 6. Then choose the best question-word for these questions about Chapter 6, and answer them.

How / What / Where

1 . . . did Hannay feel when he woke up?
2 . . . did Hannay go to escape from the police?
3 . . . did the old man do that made Hannay remember
   Scudder's story?
4 . . . story did Hannay tell the old man?
5 . . . did Hannay escape from the house?
6 . . . did Hannay hide during the day?
7 . . . did Hannay avoid the alarm bells?

Read Chapters 7 and 8, then fill in the gaps in these sentences with the correct names.

1 _____ took care of _____ when he was ill with malaria.
2 _____ had sent a letter to _____ saying that he was with a
   good friend.
3 _____ had told the police that _____ was not a murderer.
4 _____ was shot dead at seven o'clock in the evening.

5 _____ told _____ that he didn't want to arrest him.

6 _____ told the police that _____ was a murderer.

7 _____ was ill and didn't come to the meeting at _____'s house.

Read Chapter 9, then answer these questions.

Why

1 . . . were the spies clever to choose Lord Alloa?

2 . . . didn't the spy send the information by post?

3 . . . did Hannay need the book of Tide Tables?

4 . . . was high tide important?

5 . . . did Hannay think that the spy would leave from the east coast?

Before you read Chapter 10, can you guess what happens? For each sentence, circle Y (Yes) or N (No).

1 Hannay finds a house with thirty-nine steps at the Ruff. Y/N

2 Hannay finds a German fishing boat near the Ruff. Y/N

3 Hannay sees two men playing tennis very badly and realizes that they are spies. Y/N

4 Hannay doesn't recognize the spies immediately. Y/N

5 Hannay plays cards with his enemies. Y/N

6 The spies blow up the thirty-nine steps. Y/N

7 The spies escape to Germany. Y/N

8 Hannay kills one of the spies. Y/N

ACTIVITIES

After Reading

1 Complete the interview that the milkman had with the police.
   Use as many words as you like.

POLICEMAN: What time did you arrive at Mr Hannay's flat?

MILKMAN: _____.

POLICEMAN: Why did you go into the flat?

MILKMAN: _____.

POLICEMAN: You aren't wearing your coat and hat. Why did
   you take them off?

MILKMAN: _____.

POLICEMAN: That's not a very likely story! Why did he want
   your coat and hat?

MILKMAN: _____.

POLICEMAN: Did he offer you anything in return?

MILKMAN: _____.

POLICEMAN: So he bought your clothes from you, did he?

MILKMAN: _____.

POLICEMAN: What happened after the man left the flat?

MILKMAN: _____.

POLICEMAN: What did the servant do?

MILKMAN: _____.

POLICEMAN: Well, it's a good story, but I don't believe it. You
   killed the man in the study, didn't you?

MILKMAN: _____.

2 **Complete the letter that Sir Harry Andrews wrote to Sir Walter Bullivant. Choose the best word for each gap.**

Dear Sir Walter

I _____ just met a very _____ man called Richard Hannay _____ is wanted by the _____ for the Langham Place _____. But he didn't do _____, and he is in _____ trouble. The man who _____ murdered, Franklin Scudder, had _____ that some men who _____ themselves the 'Black Stone' _____ to steal secret information _____ the French and British _____ to give to the _____, who are really our _____. Scudder wrote the whole _____ in his notebook, in _____. Hannay has got the _____ and the key to _____ code, so the Black _____ want to kill him. _____ he finds some more _____ that Scudder's story is _____, he is going to _____ the British government that _____ Germans are planning to _____ Karolides, the Greek Prime _____, and start a war _____ us. I have told _____ to go to you _____ help. He will call _____ Twisdon, say the words '_____ Stone', and whistle the _____ 'Annie Laurie'. Please believe _____. I am sure that _____ is telling the truth.

_____ sincerely

Harry Andrews

3 **Match these halves of sentences and put them in the correct order to complete MacGillivray's report about the arrest of the spies. Use these words to join your sentences.**

and / and / because / because / but / so / that / that / when / where / where / who

1 _____ at half past nine Mr Hannay went in.

2 _____ the thin man had run away.

3 He stayed in the house for such a long time

4 my men and I ran into the house.

5 _____ we had put men onto the *Ariadne* an hour before.

6 My men caught the fat man,

7 _____ we could not follow the thin man.

8 Luckily, he did not escape by sea,

9 _____ one was old, one was fat, and one was thin and dark.

10 I realized that the cliff and the steps had been blown up,

11 That afternoon, Hannay discovered

12 _____ he saw three men who seemed to be English.

13 Later in the afternoon, he watched the garden of the house,

14 That evening, I told my men to hide around the house

15 _____ I heard him blow his whistle,

16 _____ I was beginning to get very worried.

17 _____ we found a house with 39 steps down to the sea.

18 _____ there was a German on a nearby yacht, the *Ariadne*.

19 Suddenly, the old man escaped from Mr Hannay,

20 _____ there was an explosion

21 Yesterday morning, Mr Hannay and I went to Bradgate,

22 _____ was holding him.

23 He ran to the wall of the room

24 He thought that they could be the criminals

4 **In this story, the characters pretend to be different people. Complete these sentences about what they pretended. Use as many words as you like.**

1 When Scudder stayed with Hannay, he pretended to be

_____.

2 When Hannay was talking to the milkman, he pretended that _____.

3 When Hannay heard that the hotel owner was bored, he pretended to _____.

4 When Hannay met Sir Harry Andrews, he pretended at first _____.

5 When two men in a big car stopped to speak to Hannay, he was pretending _____.

6 When Hannay met Marmaduke Jopley, _____.

7 When Hannay met the bald writer, _____.

8 The three Germans at Trafalgar House were _____.

9 Hannay realized that the fat man had _____.

ABOUT THE AUTHOR

John Buchan was born in Perth, Scotland, in 1875. He went to university in Oxford and while he was a student there, he started to write. After leaving university, he worked for the British government as well as continuing his writing, and he spent two years in South Africa. He was a lawyer and became a Member of Parliament in 1927. In 1935 he was made a lord, with the title Baron Tweedsmuir. At the same time, he became Governor-General of Canada (which still belonged to Britain at that time), a position that he held until his death in 1940.

He wrote many books; some were about real people, such as his lives of Sir Walter Scott and Oliver Cromwell. But he is most famous for his adventure stories, beginning with *Prester John* in 1910. Like *The Thirty-Nine Steps* (1915), these are usually exciting, fast-moving stories where brave men battle against spies and criminals. Buchan was more interested in the story than in the characters, and his books often contain long and difficult chases across country, like the one in *The Thirty-Nine Steps*. His descriptions of the countryside show his love for beautiful places like Scotland and South Africa. He wrote a total of five stories about Richard Hannay, including *Greenmantle* (1916), and several books with other heroes.

The Thirty-Nine Steps was made into a famous film by Alfred Hitchcock in 1935, and it has been filmed several times since then.

OXFORD BOOKWORMS LIBRARY

Classics • Crime & Mystery • Factfiles • Fantasy & Horror
Human Interest • Playscripts • Thriller & Adventure
True Stories • World Stories

The OXFORD BOOKWORMS LIBRARY provides enjoyable reading in English, with a wide range of classic and modern fiction, non-fiction, and plays. It includes original and adapted texts in seven carefully graded language stages, which take learners from beginner to advanced level. An overview is given on the next pages.

All Stage 1 titles are available as audio recordings, as well as over eighty other titles from Starter to Stage 6. All Starters and many titles at Stages 1 to 4 are specially recommended for younger learners. Every Bookworm is illustrated, and Starters and Factfiles have full-colour illustrations.

The OXFORD BOOKWORMS LIBRARY also offers extensive support. Each book contains an introduction to the story, notes about the author, a glossary, and activities. Additional resources include tests and worksheets, and answers for these and for the activities in the books. There is advice on running a class library, using audio recordings, and the many ways of using Oxford Bookworms in reading programmes. Resource materials are available on the website <www.oup.com/elt/bookworms>.

The *Oxford Bookworms Collection* is a series for advanced learners. It consists of volumes of short stories by well-known authors, both classic and modern. Texts are not abridged or adapted in any way, but carefully selected to be accessible to the advanced student.

You can find details and a full list of titles in the *Oxford Bookworms Library Catalogue* and *Oxford English Language Teaching Catalogues*, and on the website <www.oup.com/elt/bookworms>.

THE OXFORD BOOKWORMS LIBRARY
GRADING AND SAMPLE EXTRACTS

STARTER • 250 HEADWORDS

present simple – present continuous – imperative –
can/cannot, must – going to (future) – simple gerunds ...

Her phone is ringing – but where is it?

Sally gets out of bed and looks in her bag. No phone. She looks under the bed. No phone. Then she looks behind the door. There is her phone. Sally picks up her phone and answers it. *Sally's Phone*

STAGE 1 • 400 HEADWORDS

... past simple – coordination with *and*, *but*, *or* –
subordination with *before*, *after*, *when*, *because*, *so* ...

I knew him in Persia. He was a famous builder and I worked with him there. For a time I was his friend, but not for long. When he came to Paris, I came after him – I wanted to watch him. He was a very clever, very dangerous man. *The Phantom of the Opera*

STAGE 2 • 700 HEADWORDS

... present perfect – *will* (future) – *(don't) have to, must not, could* –
comparison of adjectives – simple *if* clauses – past continuous –
tag questions – *ask/tell* + infinitive ...

While I was writing these words in my diary, I decided what to do. I must try to escape. I shall try to get down the wall outside. The window is high above the ground, but I have to try. I shall take some of the gold with me – if I escape, perhaps it will be helpful later. *Dracula*

STAGE 3 • 1000 HEADWORDS

... should, may – present perfect continuous – *used to* – past perfect –
causative – relative clauses – indirect statements ...

Of course, it was most important that no one should see
Colin, Mary, or Dickon entering the secret garden. So Colin
gave orders to the gardeners that they must all keep away
from that part of the garden in future. ***The Secret Garden***

STAGE 4 • 1400 HEADWORDS

... past perfect continuous – passive (simple forms) –
would conditional clauses – indirect questions –
relatives with *where/when* – gerunds after prepositions/phrases ...

I was glad. Now Hyde could not show his face to the world
again. If he did, every honest man in London would be proud
to report him to the police. ***Dr Jekyll and Mr Hyde***

STAGE 5 • 1800 HEADWORDS

... future continuous – future perfect –
passive (modals, continuous forms) –
would have conditional clauses – modals + perfect infinitive ...

If he had spoken Estella's name, I would have hit him. I was so
angry with him, and so depressed about my future, that I could
not eat the breakfast. Instead I went straight to the old house.
Great Expectations

STAGE 6 • 2500 HEADWORDS

... passive (infinitives, gerunds) – advanced modal meanings –
clauses of concession, condition

When I stepped up to the piano, I was confident. It was as if I
knew that the prodigy side of me really did exist. And when I
started to play, I was so caught up in how lovely I looked that
I didn't worry how I would sound. ***The Joy Luck Club***

BOOKWORMS · THRILLER & ADVENTURE · STAGE 4

Reflex

DICK FRANCIS

Retold by Rowena Akinyemi

People who ride racehorses love the speed, the excitement, the danger – and winning the race. Philip Nore has been riding for many years and he always wants to win – but sometimes he is told to lose. Why?

And what is the mystery about the photographer, George Millace, who has just died in a car crash?

Philip Nore knows the answer to the first question, and he wants to find out the answer to the second. But as he begins to learn George Millace's secrets, he realizes that his own life is in danger.

BOOKWORMS · CRIME & MYSTERY · STAGE 4

The Big Sleep

RAYMOND CHANDLER

Retold by Rosalie Kerr

General Sternwood has four million dollars, and two young daughters, both pretty and both wild. He's an old, sick man, close to death, but he doesn't like being blackmailed. So he asks private detective Philip Marlowe to get the blackmailer off his back.

Marlowe knows the dark side of life in Los Angeles well, and nothing much surprises him. But the Sternwood girls are a lot wilder than their old father realizes. They like men, drink, drugs – and it's not just a question of blackmail.